D0099531

The Magic School Bus

Inside the Earth

The Magic School Bus
Inside the Earth

By Joanna Cole

Illustrated by Bruce Degen

Scholastic Inc.
New York · Toronto · London · Auckland · Sydney
Mexico City · New Delhi · Hong Kong · Buenos Aires

The author and illustrator wish to thank Dr. George E. Harlow,
Associate Curator, Department of Mineral Sciences
at The American Museum of Natural History,
for his assistance in preparing this book.

The author would also like to thank Dr. Peter Bower,
Professor of Geology at Barnard College,
for his helpful consultation.

ISBN-13: 978-0-590-40760-1
ISBN-10: 0-590-40760-0

54/5   7408   06/14

40 39 38 37 36 35 34 33 32   13

Printed in the U.S.A.   40

The illustrator used pen and ink, watercolor, color pencil,
and gouache for the paintings in this book.

To Michael Stone

—J.C.

To Maxwell "Mickey" Cohen and
Henry "Hank" Silverstein, who
have rocks in their heads.

—B.D.

In Ms. Frizzle's class,
we had been learning about
animals' homes
for almost a month.
We were pretty tired of it.
So everyone was happy
when Ms. Frizzle announced,
"Today we start something new."

SOMETHING NEW.
THANK GOODNESS!

GET OFF!

Beaver Lodge

PRAIRIE DOG
TOWN

7

"We are going to study
about our earth!" said Ms. Frizzle.
She put us to work
writing reports
about earth science.
"And for homework,"
she said,
"each person must find a rock
and bring it to school."

But the next day,
almost everyone had
some excuse.

I COULDN'T FIND ANY ROCKS.

I FOUND ONE, BUT MY DOG ATE IT.

YOUR DOG ATE A ROCK?

WHERE DO ROCKS COME FROM?
by Wanda

Most of the solid part of the earth is made of great masses of rock.

The small rocks that we collect are just pieces that broke off from these huge masses.

9

Only four people
had done the homework.
And Phil was the only one
who had found a real rock.

You never know
what will happen
on a trip with Ms. Frizzle.
Her new dress
was a trip in itself.
At first the old school bus
wouldn't start.
But finally we were on our way.

When we came to the field,
all the kids wanted
to get out of the bus.
But suddenly,
the bus began to spin like a top.
That sort of thing doesn't happen
on most class trips.

THE EARTH'S CRUST
by John

The outside of the earth is a shell of hard rock and soil. This shell is called the earth's crust.

When the spinning finally stopped,
some things had changed.
We all had on new clothes.
The bus had turned into
a steam shovel.
And there were shovels and picks
for every kid in the class.
"Start digging!"
yelled Ms. Frizzle.
And we began making a huge hole
right in the middle of the field.

15

THERE IS ALWAYS
ROCK UNDER YOU
by Shirley

Most of the rock in the earth's crust is covered with soil or water. But if you dig deep enough, you will find the rock. Wherever you are standing or walking or floating on earth... there is rock under you.

SOIL
ROCK

WATER ↓
ROCK

Before long—CLUNK!—we hit rock.
The Friz handed out jackhammers.
We began to break
through the hard rock.

I'M NOT USED TO MS. FRIZZLE YET!

GIVE IT TIME.

16

"Hey, these rocks have stripes," said a kid.
Ms. Frizzle explained that each stripe was a different kind of rock.

We chipped off pieces of the rocks for our class rock collection.
"These rocks are called *sedimentary* rocks, class," said Ms. Frizzle.
"There are often fossils in sedimentary rocks."

SANDSTONE IS MADE OF GRAINS OF SAND ALL PRESSED TOGETHER.

SHALE IS MADE OF MUD AND CLAY ALL PRESSED TOGETHER.

SANDSTONE FEELS GRAINY.

THIS SHALE HAS A FOSSIL OF A LEAF IN IT.

19

Wouldn't you know it?
Just when we were finding
lots of fossils,
Ms. Frizzle said,
"Back on the bus, kids."
Then, as we were driving along,
we heard rock crumbling underneath us.
Down we went.
Everything was pitch black.
And we were falling, falling, falling!

We landed with a bump.
Ms. Frizzle switched on the headlights.
We had fallen through a hole
into a huge limestone cave.
"Rain water has been dripping down
through the earth for ages,"
said Ms. Frizzle.
"The water wore away this cave
in the rock."

THE EMPIRE STATE
BUILDING IS MADE
OF LIMESTONE, TOO.

THIS WHOLE CAVE IS
MADE OF LIMESTONE.
CAN YOU FIND MORE
FOSSILS HERE?

HERE'S ONE,
MS. FRIZZLE.

KNOCK IT OFF!

We wanted to stay for a while,
but suddenly, the bus sprouted a drill.
It started boring through the rock.
Frizzie shouted, "Follow that bus!"
And down we went.

LOOK! A STALAGMITE GROWING FROM THE GROUND...

AND A STALACTITE HANGING FROM THE CEILING!

How STALAGMITES AND STALACTITES ARE FORMED
by Phil

Shapes that look like cones and icicles are formed in caves by dripping water that contains tiny invisible bits of limestone.

HOW TO REMEMBER WHICH IS WHICH:
The word stalagmite has a 'g' for ground.
The word stalactite has a 'c' for ceiling.

C

G

ANOTHER
EARTH SCIENCE WORD
by Dorothy Ann

Metamorphic comes from a word that means "to change."

The farther down we went,
the hotter it got.
The rocks were harder, too.
"These are rocks that were changed
from one kind to another kind
by heat and pressure,"
explained The Friz.
"Rocks that were changed
are called *metamorphic* rocks."

I DIDN'T KNOW ROCKS COULD CHANGE.

IT TAKES MILLIONS OF YEARS.

THIS BEAUTIFUL MARBLE USED TO BE LIMESTONE.

THEY MAKE STATUES OUT OF MARBLE.

MS. FRIZZLE
TEACHER OF THE YEAR

We had dug all the way
through the earth's crust.
It was so hot now
that Ms. Frizzle told us to
get back in the bus.

She stepped on the gas,
and the bus started *really* drilling.
Soon we were actually inside the earth.
It was hot, hot, hot!
And it got hotter and hotter
as we zoomed toward the center.

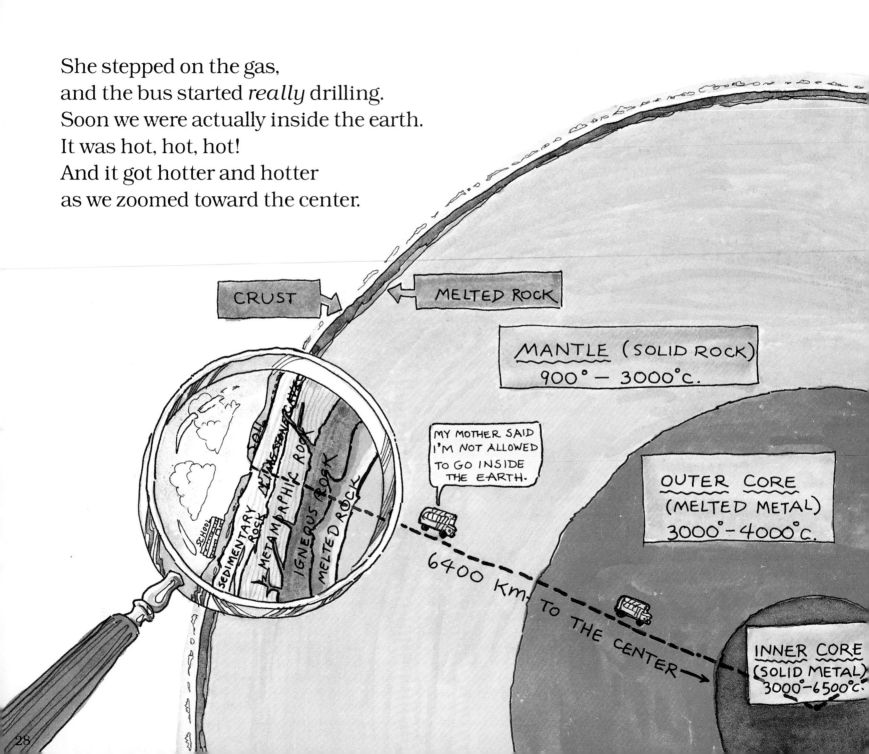

CRUST

MELTED ROCK

MANTLE (SOLID ROCK)
900° – 3000°C.

SOIL
SEDIMENTARY ROCK
METAMORPHIC ROCK
IGNEOUS ROCK
MELTED ROCK

SCHOOL

MY MOTHER SAID
I'M NOT ALLOWED
TO GO INSIDE
THE EARTH.

OUTER CORE
(MELTED METAL)
3000°–4000°C.

6400 Km. TO THE CENTER →

INNER CORE
(SOLID METAL)
3000–6500°C.

We were glad when Ms. Frizzle
headed out again.
We reached the earth's crust
and drove straight up through
a tunnel of black rock.
It was great to see the sky.

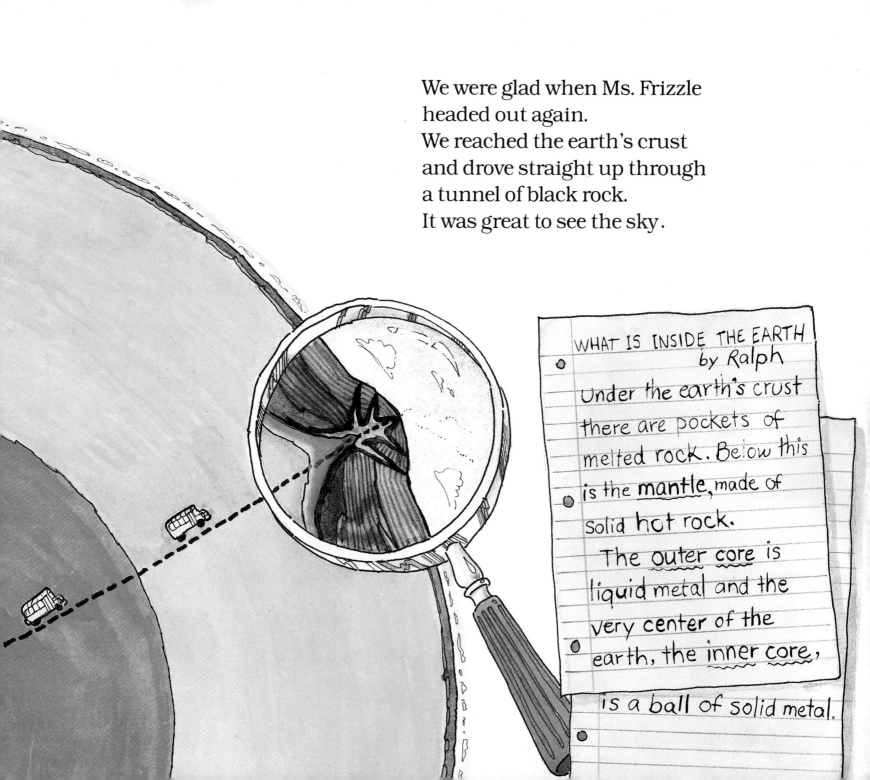

WHAT IS INSIDE THE EARTH
by Ralph

Under the earth's crust
there are pockets of
melted rock. Below this
is the **mantle**, made of
solid hot rock.

The outer core is
liquid metal and the
very center of the
earth, the inner core,
is a ball of solid metal.

Then we looked around.
We had come out on an island
in the middle of the ocean!
"Isn't this wonderful, class?"
said Frizzie.
"We've driven right up
on a volcanic island!"
It didn't look like much.
But if Ms. Frizzle was right,
the whole island was one big volcano!

30

We were nervous, but Ms. Frizzle made us
collect some rocks.
She said they had all
hardened from melted rock that had come
out of the volcano.
Then, suddenly, we heard rumblings from below.

VOLCANOES MAKE
NEW LAND   by Arnold

The material that comes
out of a volcano is
melted rock called lava.
When lava cools, it
hardens into new rock.
In time, soil forms
on the rock and plants
can grow.

I DIDN'T KNOW
VOLCANOES
COULD BE USEFUL!

We scrambled into the bus.
The Friz turned the ignition key
and stepped on the gas.
Nothing happened.
The bus would not start!
We thought we were goners!

UH-OH

Red-hot lava came streaming
out of the volcano.
Some of it shot into the air
like a fountain.
Some of it flowed over the land
like a river.
Our bus went along with it—
right into the sea.

When the red-hot lava hit the water,
it made a huge cloud of steam.
All we could see was white.
We seemed to be rising
with the steam and floating along.
No one knows how long
we floated in the cloud…

but when it finally cleared,
we were back in the school parking lot.

It had been a weird trip,
but we *did* get
a great rock collection
for our classroom.

Rock COLLECTION
by MS. FRIZZLE'S CLASS

NOT A ROCK!

SHIRLEY'S ROCK
LIMESTONE

TYPE: Sedimentary (formed from shells)
USES: Buildings, chalk, cement, fertilizer

Amanda Jane's rock
MARBLE

TYPE: Metamorphic (formed from limestone)
USES: Statues, monuments, buildings

Phoebe's rock
SHALE

TYPE: Sedimentary (formed by mud)
USES: Ground up and mixed with limestone for cement, brick

Wanda's rock
GRANITE

TYPE: Igneous
USES: Monuments, buildings, Curbstones

JOHN'S rock
SLATE

TYPE: Metamorphic (formed from shale)
USES: Roofing tile, flagstones, chalkboards

Michael's rock
SANDSTONE

TYPE: Sedimentary (formed by sand)
USES: Buildings, grindstones

MOLLY'S rock
BASALT

TYPE: Igneous (Volcanic)
USES: Road Building

Rachel's rock
OBSIDIAN

TYPE: Igneous (Volcanic)
USES: Decoration, Indian Arrowheads

Florrie's rock
PUMICE

TYPE: Igneous (Volcanic)
USES: Ground-up in Scouring powder

Phil's rock
QUARTZITE

TYPE: Metamorphic (formed from sandstone)
USES: Millstones for grinding grain, road building

A WORD WITH THE AUTHOR AND THE ARTIST

The first reader of this book called to complain. He said the book was full of mistakes. We recorded the conversation to help you decide which things are true and which were put in to make the story more exciting.

READER: This book is full of mistakes!

AUTHOR: It is not!

ARTIST: Everything in this book is absolutely true and really happened.

READER: What about the beaver lodge on page 7?

AUTHOR: Oh, that. Well, I guess that *would* be too messy in a real classroom.

READER: And the beehive?

ARTIST: That, too. But everything else is fact.

READER: Oh, come *on!* You mean kids can use jackhammers (page 16), and a bus can change into a steam shovel (page 14) and a drill (page 23)?

AUTHOR: Well, er, now that you mention it, that is not really possible.

READER: And do you expect me to believe that a bus can go through the center of the earth (page 28)?

ARTIST: Yes....

AUTHOR: Maybe....

ARTIST: Well, actually, no. The bus couldn't do that, either.

AUTHOR: Even if a bus *could* drill its way through, the distance is so long that the trip would take months, even years.

READER: And what about the heat?

AUTHOR: Okay, okay! It's white-hot in the center of the earth. The bus would be burned up in a minute.

READER: Isn't it kind of ridiculous to say that air-conditioning would help?

AUTHOR: Gee, you're a tough cookie! Okay, you're right. Air-conditioning could not make any difference in that kind of heat.

READER: And the bus could not flow in lava and go up in a cloud of steam (pages 33-34)?

ARTIST: Give us a break! You're right again. That's not true, either.

READER: But you said *everything* was true!

AUTHOR: Everything *else* is. Honest!

READER: Everything else is true? There truly are sedimentary, metamorphic, and igneous rocks?

AUTHOR: Certainly!

READER: And lava really does harden into new rock?

ARTIST: Oh, yes.

READER: And what about Ms. Frizzle's clothing?

AUTHOR: That *is* hard to believe, but it's true.

ARTIST: She really does dress that way!

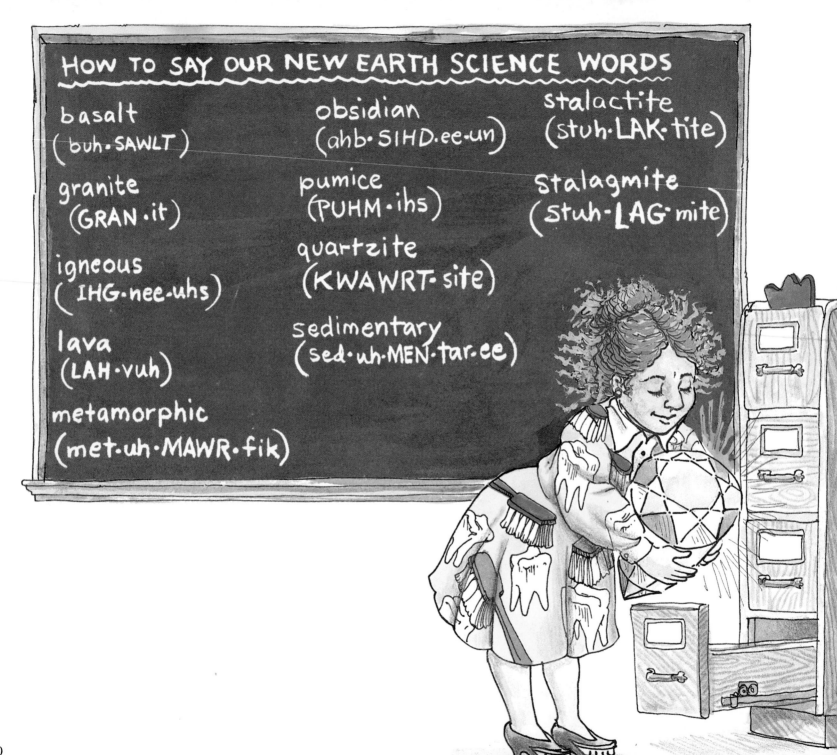

HOW TO SAY OUR NEW EARTH SCIENCE WORDS

basalt
(buh·SAWLT)

granite
(GRAN·it)

igneous
(IHG·nee·uhs)

lava
(LAH·vuh)

metamorphic
(met·uh·MAWR·fik)

obsidian
(ahb·SIHD·ee·un)

pumice
(PUHM·ihs)

quartzite
(KWAWRT·site)

sedimentary
(sed·uh·MEN·tar·ee)

stalactite
(stuh·LAK·tite)

stalagmite
(stuh·LAG·mite)